ALISON HOLST'S
More Marvellous
MUFFINS

BY SIMON AND ALISON HOLST

First published in 1997 by Hyndman Publishing PO Box 5017, Dunedin
ISBN 1-877168-10-6
© TEXT: Simon & Alison Holst

DESIGNER: Rob Di Leva

PHOTOGRAPHER: Lindsay Keats

HOME ECONOMISTS: Simon & Alison Holst, Jane Ritchie

PRINTING: Tablet Colour Print

The recipes in this book have been carefully tested by the authors. The publisher and the authors have made every effort to ensure that the instructions are accurate and safe, but they cannot accept liability for any resulting injury or loss or damage to property whether direct or consequential.

Because ovens and microwave ovens vary so much, you should take the cooking times suggested in recipes as guides only. The first time you make a recipe, check it at intervals to make sure it is not cooking faster, or more slowly than expected.

Always follow the detailed instructions given by manufacturers of your appliances and equipment, rather than the more general instructions given in these recipes.

Acknowledgements

We would like to thank the firms who provided us with the following food and products.

ALISON'S CHOICE Dried fruit, nuts, seeds, etc.

BENNICK'S POULTRY FARM, BULLER RD, LEVIN Fresh eggs

CHAMPION All the flours and wheatgerm used in these recipes

CHEFMATE Non-stick spray

EDMONDS Baking soda and baking powder

EMERSON'S BREWERY Beer

EMPIRE FOODSTUFFS Dried herbs and spices

FERNDALE Parmesan cheese

FLEMING'S Oatbran, bran flakes and rolled oats

GALAXY Creamy blue cheese

GENOESE FOODS Pesto

HEINZ-WATTIE Canned products

LUPI Olive oil and Balsamic vinegar

SUREBRAND Teflon muffin liners

TARARUA Grated cheese and dairy products

The tableware in the photographs was supplied by the following Wellington stores:

PAGE 23   Breakfast china from Theme

PAGE 24   China from Levene

PAGE 42   Mugs from Theme

PAGE 52   Teapot from Levene

Contents

Measures for muffins

To get the best results from our recipes you need to measure your ingredients carefully.

We have measured dry ingredients and liquids with metric cups and spoons.

A set of plastic or metal metric measuring cups (where 1 cup holds 250ml) helps you measure your ingredients quickly and easily. We use the 1 cup, ½ cup and ¼ cup measures. We do not use a ⅓ cup measure, and if you own one, suggest it is better hidden, so you do not use it instead of your ¼ cup measure, by mistake!

When you measure flour, fill the cup from the set lightly, and level it off with the edge of a knife, without any shaking or banging, since this packs down the flour and means that you use too much. (Packing too much flour in a cup is a very common mistake and means that your muffin mixture will be too thick and stodgy.)

Measure liquids right to the rim of these single capacity measuring cups, or use a clear plastic graduated cup or jug.

We give most butter quantities by weight. The markings on butter packs are accurate enough, apart from the markings at each end of the pack. We measure small quantities of butter in spoons – one level tablespoon of butter weighs 15g.

Use a set of metric measuring spoons. Our metric tablespoon holds 15 millilitres, and our teaspoon five millilitres.

The cup and spoon measures in this book are level, unless otherwise stated. A heaped spoon holds twice as much as a level one, and will upset the balance of the ingredients used in a recipe. Level measures for baking powder and baking soda are especially important.

Golden syrup, honey and treacle are the exceptions to our "level measures" rule. We find it more practical to use rounded (metal) household spoonfuls of these. Heat the spoon with very hot water first.

We use the following abbreviations:

cm	centimetre
C	Celsius
ml	millilitre
g	gram
tsp	teaspoon
Tbsp	tablespoon

Why make more muffins?

In "Marvellous Muffins" I thought that I had covered the range of muffins pretty well. I was wrong! Since then, thousands of keen muffin cooks have "talked muffins" with me, often asking if I have recipes for other muffins which they have tasted, and would like to make.

When I first thought of writing another muffin book, I asked my 12 year old granddaughter, Elizabeth, what she would choose at a muffin bar or would like to make herself. She staggered me with more than 100 mouth-watering suggestions! With these in mind, my son Simon and I started experimenting. Simon favoured relatively short ingredient lists and simple mixing methods, so inexperienced cooks with limited equipment could make our muffins too, and added still more innovative flavour combinations. This book then, has input from three Holst generations, so has been great fun for me!

As I wrote in my first muffin book, muffins are SO versatile! They are a treat for a late weekend breakfast and the perfect accompaniment for morning or afternoon tea or coffee. Savoury muffins can be the main part of a lunch or light weekend evening meal, and richer or fresh fruit muffins make wonderful desserts. Mini-muffins are at home at cocktail parties, and muffins of all flavours and sizes are a welcome addition to packed lunches and picnic meals.

But, that's not all! A basket of muffins will thank a teacher, greet a new neighbour, welcome home the mother of a new baby, cheer an ill or elderly acquaintance, and help raise funds for your church, kindy or school, too.

Is it easy to make really good muffins? Yes! and usually in a short time, without complicated equipment. If you want only one baking specialty, make it muffins.

Are muffins expensive to make? Most are not, and those which sound luxurious and expensive usually contain only small amounts of "gourmet" ingredients.

Will your family get sick of muffins? Mine haven't yet, because muffin recipes vary so much. They need never become boring, because it is so easy to "ring the changes".

It takes only a little practice to become a muffin expert – to get the "feel" of muffin mixtures, and to make really marvellous muffins every time you make a batch. I hope you enjoy this book even more than my first one, and that you will be encouraged to try many of our delicious muffins, then invent some of your own. Elizabeth, Simon and I hope you and your families enjoy our ideas!

What size and shape should muffins be?

Muffin pans vary in size. Whatever pans you buy, make sure they have a good non-stick finish, since some muffin mixtures stick badly!

Medium-Sized Muffins

Most widely used are muffin trays which make twelve medium-sized muffins. (The twelve depressions, if filled with water, hold 4 cupfuls altogether.) Most of the recipes in this book will make 12 muffins this size, with about a quarter-cup measure of mixture into each muffin hole, but you can put more than this and make 8–9 muffins instead.

You can also buy muffin trays with six holes the size of those above. These fit in most bench-top ovens, and are also handy if you have a little mixture left over, and want to make a few more muffins.

Mini-Muffins

Mini-muffin tins are fun! Hardly any one will refuse one of these little muffins which are about half the size of those above. (12 mini-muffin pans, if filled with water, hold 1½ cupfuls.) A mixture making 12 medium muffins makes 22–30 mini-muffins. Mini-muffins usually take 2 minutes less than medium muffins do to cook.

Mini-muffin trays usually fit in bench-top ovens.

Monster Muffins

Monster-muffin (Texan Muffin) trays hold six muffins, each twice the size of medium muffins. (The tray of six holds 5 cups of water.) These muffins usually take 2–4 minutes longer to cook than medium muffins. These pans are not widely available. We don't use them as much as we used to, because it is too easy to eat more than we should!

Small Cake Pans

You CAN make muffins in (shallower) small cake pans, but don't expect such good results. The muffins will be flatter and crustier than normal.

Gem Irons

If you have gem irons tucked away in a bottom cupboard, by all means try cooking your muffins in them. Heat the irons in the oven as it warms. Put the hot irons on a heat-resistant surface, brush quickly with melted butter, or spray well with non-stick spray, then drop in the mixture from the side of a dessert spoon. The cooking time will be shorter than for medium muffins.

Paper cases and Teflon Muffins Liners

Paper cases are sometimes used for muffins which are to be sold or handled a lot. They are useful for muffins which stick to non-stick metal surfaces, and are very helpful for microwaved muffins which often stick badly. Teflon liners are useful for making a few microwaved muffins. Muffins baked in cases do not have an appealing crust, however.

Non-stick sprays

We find these invaluable, even on non-stick trays. However, always follow the tray manufacturer's instructions. At least one company does not recommend the use of non-stick sprays on the non-stick muffin pans they make.

To make marvellous muffins

The cooks' tips on this page should help you make perfect muffins!

First, combine the dry ingredients in a bowl big enough to mix everything. As long as you toss them really well with a dry whisk or fork, you don't need to sieve or sift them.

Next, mix the liquids. Heat butter just until liquid in a pot or microwave oven, add the other liquids, then the egg, and mix with a fork, beater or whisk. Especially in cold weather, don't leave this mixture to stand until the butter solidifies again.

You can add extra ingredients to the liquids or dry ingredients. It is often better to add them to the liquids.

The way you mix the dry and wet mixtures together is vital. Combine all ingredients at once rather than adding them gradually. FOLD EVERYTHING TOGETHER, MIXING AS LITTLE AS POSSIBLE. (We use a flexible straight-bladed stirrer/spreader.) Slowly bring your stirrer, scraper, fork or spoon down the side of the bowl and under the mixture, then up through the middle of it, turning bowl and repeating until no pockets of flour are left. STOP MIXING WHILE THE MIXTURE STILL LOOKS ROUGH AND LUMPY. It doesn't matter if a little flour is still visible. Overmixing toughens muffins and makes them rise in peaks instead of being gently rounded.

If your muffin mixture looks too thick (too much flour?), thin it with extra milk, water or juice before you have finished mixing.

Muffins often stick to baking pans, so use pans with a non-stick finish, which have been cleaned without scratching, and coat with non-stick spray unless manufacturer's instructions forbid this.

Spoon the batter into the prepared pans, helping the mixture off with another spoon. Try to put one spoonful in each pan. Let the mixture mound naturally – do not smooth or flatten its surface.

Bake muffins at a high temperature until they have browned attractively and the centres spring back when pressed. At this stage a skewer pushed into the centre comes out clean, too. Overcooked muffins are dry, with hard crusts. Suggested cooking times are only a guide, since ovens vary so much. Our muffins were cooked in ovens with fans. Without a fan, you may need higher temperatures or longer cooking times.

After cooking, let muffins stand in their pans for 3–4 minutes. They loosen themselves in this time! Press down gently on the edges of a muffin with several fingers of one hand, and twist slightly. As soon as the muffin will turn freely, lift it out, and let it cool on a rack.

In general, muffins are best served warm, soon after baking. They will stay warm for some time, without going soggy, in a napkin-lined basket. Reheat when necessary (taking care not to overheat) in a microwave oven, or in a paper bag at about 150°C in a conventional oven.

If you are freezing muffins, bag, seal and freeze them quickly, soon after they have cooled to room temperature. Use within a few weeks, warming them before serving them.

Easy Cheesy Muffins

Some years ago, during a bakers' strike, an easy bread made from self-raising flour and beer "did the rounds".
Starting with the same basic ingredients, you can make wonderful cheesy muffins!

2 cups Champion Self-Raising Flour
2 cups (200g) grated tasty cheese

1 large egg
1 cup lager or beer
about 2 Tbsp chutney, optional

Mix the flour and grated cheese together in a large bowl.

Using a fork, beat the egg enough to thoroughly mix the white and yolk. Add the lager or beer (which can be flat or bubbly) and stir to mix briefly, then pour the mixture onto the flour and cheese.

Fold together until most of the flour is dampened, but do not overmix. (See details of mixing and baking on page 7.) If you like the idea, drizzle your favourite chutney over the surface, and fold it in lightly so that it stays in streaks.

Spoon the mixture into 12 buttered or sprayed medium-sized muffin pans.

Bake at 220°C for 10–15 minutes, until nicely browned, and until the centres spring back when pressed.

YIELD: 12 generous medium-sized muffins or 24 mini-muffins. **SERVE:** Warm or cold the day they are made, or reheated next day. Very popular for lunch. Warm mini muffins make excellent party snacks.

Mexican Muffins

The flavours we love in Mexican foods go very well in tasty, substantial muffins, too.

*2 cups Champion High Grade
 or Standard Plain Flour*
4 tsp Edmonds Baking Powder
1 cup grated tasty cheese

*300g can (1 cup) Tomato Salsa
 or 1 cup Mexican Spiced Tomatoes*
*1 cup drained canned Mexican Corn
 or Whole Kernel Corn*
1 cup sour cream
1 large egg
*¼–½ tsp each chili powder, cumin,
 and oreganum*
½ tsp salt

½ cup grated tasty cheese, optional
paprika, optional

Measure the flour and baking powder into a large bowl. Add the grated cheese and toss everything together lightly.

Measure whichever tomato and (drained) corn you are using into another bowl and add the sour cream and egg.

Add the seasonings, using the smaller amounts (or none) if you have used the salsa and Mexican corn which are already seasoned. Mix everything with a fork until well blended.

Pour the liquid mixture into the dry ingredients and fold everything together until the flour is barely dampened. Do not over-mix! (See details on page 7.)

Spoon the mixture into 12 prepared (sprayed or buttered) medium-sized muffin pans. Top the uncooked muffins with the second measure of cheese and paprika if you like.

Bake for 12–15 minutes at 220° C, or until firm when pressed in the centre.

NOTE: A can of Watties Tomato Salsa is a good choice for this recipe because it contains exactly a cup.

YIELD: 12 (generous) medium muffins or 24 mini-muffins. **SERVE:** Good warm, alone or with a green salad for lunch, or served alongside your favourite Tex Mex food.

Hawaiian Ham Muffins

*Shut your eyes and be transported to a tropical island with white sands, waving palms, soft guitar music and undulating hips…
or more prosaically, remember that "Hawaiian" is the name used for a combination of ham, pineapple and cheese!*

2 cups Champion Standard Plain Flour
4 tsp Edmonds Baking Powder
½ tsp salt
about 100g ham or ham pieces, diced
1½ cups grated tasty cheese
2 spring onions, chopped

300g can crushed pineapple
about ¾ cup coconut cream or milk
1 large egg

Measure the dry ingredients into a large bowl. Add the diced ham and grated cheese. Chop and add the green leaves as well as the white part of the spring onions, and toss everything together until evenly combined, using a fork.

Drain the pineapple, reserving the juice. Make the juice up to 1 cup with coconut cream or milk. Put the crushed pineapple, liquid and egg in a smaller bowl and mix until well combined, again using the fork.

Pour the liquid into the flour mixture, and fold together until the flour is moistened, taking care to avoid overmixing. (Read mixing and baking details on page 7.)

Spoon the mixture into 12 medium or 24 mini-muffin pans which have been sprayed or lightly buttered. Top with a little extra grated cheese if you like.

Bake at 210°C for 12–15 minutes, or until tops and sides are brown, and the centres spring back when lightly pressed.

YIELD: 12 medium or 24 mini-muffins. **SERVE:** As party finger food; with a hot or cold drink at any time of day; as the main part of a weekend brunch or lunch.

Mediterranean Muffins

Perfect for a trouble-free light lunch outside on the patio, or under a shady tree on a hot day.
Add a glass of wine and whatever fresh fruit seems most appealing, and relax!

2 cups Champion Self-Raising Flour
½ tsp salt

about ¼ cup sundried tomatoes
about ¼ cup pitted black olives
100g feta cheese, cubed
2 Tbsp basil pesto
¾ cup milk
1 large egg
¼ cup olive oil

Measure the flour and salt into a large bowl and toss with a fork.

Place the sundried tomatoes (roughly equivalent to 4–5 whole tomatoes) and olives into the bowl of a food processor. Process briefly until these are chopped into smallish pieces. Add the cubed feta, pesto, milk, egg and olive oil, then process briefly to combine everything.

Pour the liquid mixture into the flour and stir gently until all the flour is moistened.

Spoon the mixture into 12 medium or 24 mini-muffin pans which have been buttered or sprayed. (Top each with a couple of extra slices of olive if you like.)

Bake at 220°C for 10–12 minutes, until the tops are golden and the centres spring back when pressed.

VARIATIONS: Instead of food processing, finely chop the sun-dried tomatoes, olives and feta cheese by hand, then mix well with the pesto, milk, egg and oil using a fork. Instead of being pinkish, these will have flecks of colour through them.

If preferred, leave out the feta and serve topped with slices of feta or with a 1cm cube of feta pushed into each medium muffin, just before baking.

YIELD: 12 medium or 24 mini-muffins. SERVE: Warm or cold. The olive flavour is more pronounced when muffins are cold.

Kumara, Bacon & Onion Muffins

Picture opposite

There is something memorable about these muffins! They have a mild but definite flavour and texture, and are a very popular addition to luncheon soup and salad buffets, especially when overseas visitors are present.

2 Tbsp oil
2 rashers (100g) lean bacon, chopped
1 small onion

2 cups Champion Self-Raising Flour
1 cup grated tasty cheese
1 tsp mild curry powder
1/2 tsp salt

1 cup milk
1 large egg
1 cup (200g) roughly mashed cooked
 kumara*

Heat the oil in medium-sized frypan. Cook the chopped bacon and diced onion in the oil until the bacon begins to brown.

Meanwhile, measure the flour, grated cheese, curry powder and salt into a large bowl. Toss well with a fork to mix.

In another bowl mix the milk and egg with the fork until blended, then stir in the roughly mashed kumara, and mix again, leaving some chunky pieces.

Tip the cooked bacon and onion, then the kumara mixture into the flour. Gently fold everything together until the flour is moistened. Do not overmix. (See mixing and baking details on page 7.)

Spoon the mixture into 12 lightly buttered or sprayed medium-sized muffin pans or 24 mini-muffin pans. Bake at 200°C for 12–15 minutes, or until golden brown on top and firm when pressed in the centre.

*Use Golden Kumara if possible, since they give these muffins a definite gold colour. For easy preparation, scrub about 300g of kumara, cut off any hairy protrusions, then microwave for 4–5 minutes, until the flesh in the thickest part "gives" when gently squeezed. When cool, peel off skin and mash roughly.

YIELD: 12 medium or 24 mini-muffins. SERVE: See above. Good flavour when hot, warm or cold. Buttering is not necessary.

Pizza Muffins

Picture opposite

If your family and friends like pizza, (and who doesn't), I am sure that you will find that these muffins
"go down a treat" for lunch or with coffee.

2 cups grated tasty cheese
2 cups Champion High-Grade or
    Standard Plain flour
3 tsp Edmonds Baking Powder
1 Tbsp sugar
1 spring onion, chopped
50g salami, finely chopped
$\frac{1}{2}$ tsp oreganum, crumbled

1 Tbsp tomato paste
3 Tbsp water
1 cup milk
1 large egg

Optional Topping
$\frac{1}{2}$ medium tomato, finely chopped
about $\frac{1}{2}$ cup grated cheese
2–3 slices salami, chopped

Measure the grated cheese, whichever flour you have or like, baking powder and sugar into a large bowl. Add the chopped leaves and stem of the spring onion, the finely chopped salami and oreganum, then stir lightly to combine.

Using a fork, mix the tomato paste and water until smooth in a medium-sized bowl. Add the milk and egg, and beat with the fork until well combined.

Pour the liquids into the flour mixture and fold together until the flour is moistened. Take care not to overmix!

Spoon the mixture into 12 medium-sized well-sprayed or buttered muffin pans, or into 24 mini-muffin pans.

If you have the time and inclination, add a topping for extra visual appeal. Remove and discard the seeds from the tomato and dice the flesh finely. Sprinkle a few pieces of tomato, a few shreds of grated cheese and a couple of pieces of salami on to each muffin.

Bake at 220°C for 12 minutes, or until lightly browned on top and firm when pressed in the middle.

NOTE: Chop chunks of salami into small pieces in a food processor, if available.

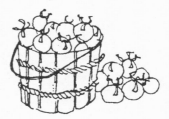

YIELD: 12 medium or 24 min-muffins. **SERVE:** Irresistible hot from the oven, but the flavour is even better when cold.

Ham & Whole Grain Mustard Muffins

Team these with a bowl of warming pea soup or creamy vegetable soup for lunch on wintery day, or enjoy them with a salad in summer, to use the last of the Christmas ham. Mini-sized muffins are great served with drinks, too.

about 100g ham pieces, chopped
2 cups Champion Standard Plain Flour
4 tsp Edmonds Baking Powder
¼ tsp salt, optional
1–1½ cups grated tasty cheese
2 spring onions, chopped

1 cup milk
about 2 Tbsp whole grain mustard
1 large egg

Chop the ham into small pieces and put in a large bowl. Measure in the flour and baking powder, and the salt if you are using the smaller amounts of ham and cheese. Add the grated cheese and chopped spring onions (green and white parts), then toss all these ingredients together thoroughly, separating the pieces of ham, cheese and onion.

Whisk together the milk, grainy mustard and egg in a small bowl. (You may wish to vary the quantity of mustard according to your taste and the heat of the mustard you are using.) Tip the liquid mixture into the dry ingredients, then fold them in, taking care not to overmix, until the flour is moistened and the mixture is reasonably uniform. Do not overmix. (Read mixing and baking details on page 7.)

Spoon the mixture into 12 sprayed or lightly buttered medium sized muffin pans and bake at 210°C for 12–15 minutes, until the centres spring back when lightly pressed.

NOTE: For small cocktail muffins use more ham, cheese and mustard. Add up to ¼ cup chopped fresh herbs if you like.

YIELD: 10–12 medium muffins, depending on the size you want, or 20–24 mini-muffins. SERVE: Flavour is best when muffins are cold.

Spicy Corn & Cheese Muffins

These muffins have an interesting flavour and texture and may be seasoned to suit your taste. They are as good with a bowl of warming soup in autumn and winter as they are for a summer picnic, or with a spring luncheon salad.

1 cup creamed corn
2 large eggs
½ cup milk

2 cups Champion Standard Plain Flour
4 tsp Edmonds Baking Powder
¾ tsp salt
1½ cups (150g) grated tasty cheese
1 tsp ground cumin, optional
½ tsp oreganum, optional
½ tsp chili powder, optional

Measure the corn, eggs and milk into a fairly large bowl and mix with a fork until combined. (The amount of corn does not need to be exact. If you are using up corn left in a can add a little extra or less milk to make your muffins the right wetness.)

Measure the remaining ingredients into a large bowl, leaving out or using more or less of the last three flavourings according to your taste. (If you like, measure the dry ingredients and chunks of weighed cheese into a food processor and chop finely, instead of grating it.)

Tip the dry ingredients (with the cheese) into the corn mixture and fold together until evenly dampened but not smooth. Add a little extra milk if the mixture is not moist enough.

Divide the mixture between 12 medium or 24 mini-muffin pans which have been buttered or sprayed. Top each with a piece of cheese or some grated cheese and a sprinkling of paprika. (Read mixing and baking details on page 7.)

Bake at 220°C for 9–12 minutes, until the centres spring back when pressed and the sides and tops are golden brown.

VARIATION: Add the chopped leaves and stems of 2 spring onions if not using the spices.

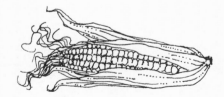

YIELD: 8–12 medium or 20–24 mini-muffins, depending on the size of each. SERVE: Best of all served straight from the oven, but good cool and cold, too.

Bacon Brunch Muffins

Get the weekend off to a good start, pleasing your family or friends by serving a basket of bacon-flavoured muffins and a bowl of fresh fruit salad (with yoghurt) for brunch or breakfast.

2–3 Tbsp oil
4 rashers (200g) lean bacon

2 cups Champion Standard Plain Flour
4 tsp Edmonds Baking Powder
½ tsp salt
1½ cups grated tasty cheese
pinch cayenne or chili powder, optional

1 large egg
1 cup milk

Put the oil and chopped (derinded) bacon in a large pan and cook until the bacon is lightly browned.

Measure the flour, baking powder, salt, grated cheese and optional flavouring into a bowl large enough to mix all the ingredients. (Use absolutely level teaspoons of baking powder or the muffins will taste of soda.)

Using a fork, mix the milk and egg together in a suitable small container. Add the cooked bacon and any pan drippings, with the milk and egg mixture to the bowl of dry ingredients. Fold together until the flour is wet, taking great care not to overmix. (See mixing and baking details on page 7.)

Spoon the mixture into 12 medium or 24 mini-muffin pans which have been buttered or sprayed.

Bake at 220°C for 10–12 minutes, or until centres spring back when pressed.

NOTE: Less bacon means less flavour! Don't scrimp – use an extra rasher (and no salt) if you have it!

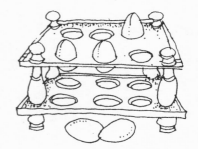

YIELD: 12 medium or 24 mini-muffins. SERVE: Good warm or cold. Mini muffins certainly don't need buttering.

Blue Cheese, Pear (& Walnut) Muffins

This recipe is for people who are looking for a muffin which is a little different, and who enjoy the flavours of blue cheese and pears together. The optional walnuts add a lovely crunch and are a good idea if you have high quality nuts on hand.

1 cup Champion Standard Plain Flour
1 cup Champion Wholemeal Flour
¼–½ cup chopped walnuts, optional
4 tsp Edmonds Baking Powder
1 Tbsp sugar
½ tsp salt

100g wedge of creamy blue cheese
1 large egg
2 medium-sized ripe pears or 1 cup
    chopped drained canned pears
½ cup milk

Measure the first six ingredients into a large bowl and toss together thoroughly, using a fork.

Again using the fork, mash the blue cheese into another bowl, then add the egg and mix and mash again. Stir in the milk, then coarsely grate or very finely chop the quartered, unpeeled fresh pears and stir them in too. Drained canned pears should be chopped into pieces about pea size. (Aim to have some small pieces of cheese and pear – not a perfectly smooth mixture.)

Add the liquid to the flour mixture, and fold together until the flour is dampened. Avoid overmixing. (If the mixture seems drier than a normal muffin mixture, add a little extra milk.)

Spoon the mixture into 9–12 sprayed or lightly buttered medium muffin pans and bake at 210°C for about 12 minutes, or until browned on top and firm when pressed in the centre.

NOTE: We used Galaxy creamy blue cheese in these muffins.

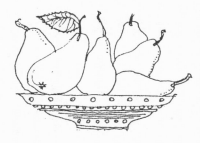

YIELD: 9–12 medium muffins. SERVE: For best flavour and texture eat these muffins cold, the day they are made. Try them with a cup of coffee or a glass of wine, with no other food!

Zucchini & Parmesan Muffins

These muffins, flecked with pale green, are light, pretty and fresh tasting, perfect for serving on a summer's day. You'll find them especially appealing if your family has seen enough zucchini from the garden on their dinner plates!

2 cups Champion Standard Plain Flour
4 tsp Edmonds Baking Powder
½ tsp salt
black pepper to taste
1 cup grated tasty cheese
¼ cup grated Parmesan

¾ cup milk
2 eggs
3 zucchini, grated (250g)

Sift or fork together the flour, baking powder and salt in a large bowl. Grind in black pepper to taste then add the grated cheeses and stir to combine.

Using a fork, whisk together the milk and eggs, then add the grated zucchini. Tip this mixture into the bowl of dry ingredients.

Fold the mixture together, taking care not to over-mix. As soon as all the flour is moistened, spoon the mixture into 12 lightly buttered or sprayed medium-sized muffin pans or 24 mini-muffin pans.

Bake at 210°C for 12–15 minutes, or until the tops are golden and the muffins spring back when pressed in the centre.

NOTE: If you like freshly ground pepper, use plenty in these muffins!

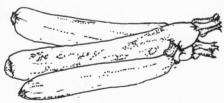

YIELD: 12 medium or 24 mini-muffins. SERVE:Nice cold or warm. Mini muffins do not need any spread. Enjoy larger muffins as they are or topped with sliced tomato and herbs. Good for picnic lunches.

Herbed Chicken & Cranberry Muffins

Make these unusual, savoury muffins to use up the last of a festive chicken (or turkey) or a smoked chicken breast.
If preferred, leave out the chicken and make mini-muffins to serve with roast poultry, instead of stuffing and cranberry sauce.

2 cups Champion Standard Plain Flour
3 tsp Edmonds Baking Powder
½ tsp salt
¼ cup chopped fresh herbs
    (half parsley, half thyme or
    marjoram etc.)
black pepper
1 cup (150g) chopped cooked chicken

75g butter
½ medium onion, diced
225g jar whole cranberry sauce

1 large egg
½ cup milk

Sift the flour, baking powder and salt into a large bowl. Add the chopped fresh herbs, freshly ground black pepper to taste and the chopped cooked (plain or smoked) chicken. Toss together until evenly mixed.

Melt the butter in a medium sized frypan, add the diced onion and cook for 2–3 minutes until the onion is soft. Reduce the heat and spoon in the cranberry sauce. Heat, stirring gently until the sauce has just melted.

Whisk together the egg and milk, and add this, along with the cranberry mixture, to the dry ingredients.

Gently fold everything together until the flour just is dampened. Take care not to overmix. (See mixing and baking details on page 7.)

Spoon the mixture into 10 medium or 24 mini-muffin pans which have been sprayed or lightly buttered, and bake at 200°C for 12 minutes or until lightly browned and firm when pressed in the centre.

VARIATION: Add ¼–½ cup of dried cranberries.

YIELD: 10 medium or 24 mini-muffins. **SERVE:** Warm, with a salad, for lunch. If made without the chicken, serve warm with roast poultry. Good at a buffet meal.

Spiced Muesli & Honey Muffins

— *Picture opposite*

These tender, soft-textured, delicious muffins are deservedly popular, even with those doubtful about all the "good for you" ingredients in them! Use a tasty, interesting fruity muesli — two muffins contain a good sized serving of it.

1 cup Champion High Grade
   or Standard Plain Flour
1 cup Champion Wholemeal Flour
2 cups toasted muesli
¾ tsp salt
½ tsp Edmonds Baking Soda
1 tsp Edmonds Baking Powder
2 tsp mixed spice

½ cup canola oil
½ cup runny honey
½ cup natural (or fruity) yoghurt
½ cup orange juice
1 large egg
1 tsp vanilla

Measure the flours and muesli into a large bowl. Measure into a sieve, then sift in the salt, baking soda, baking powder and mixed spice. Combine well, using your fingers or a fork.

In another bowl, using a fork, mix together the oil, honey (which has been warmed if necessary), yoghurt, orange juice, egg and vanilla.

Pour the liquid into the dry ingredients and fold everything together until just combined. Do not overmix (see page 7 for mixing and baking details). Don't worry if the mixture seems very wet, since the muesli absorbs some liquid as it cooks.

Spoon the mixture into 12 sprayed or oiled muffin pans and bake at 200°C for 12–15 minutes, until firm when pressed in the centre and lightly browned.

NOTES: If you have it, use high grade (bread) flour rather than plain flour, since it has the ability to "hold up" all the other ingredients very well.

We used Alison's Choice Toasted Muesli in our excellent and popular muffins!

YIELD: 12 medium or 24 mini-muffins. **SERVE:** Hot from the oven (or reheated) for breakfast, morning coffee or brunch.

Blueberry Bran Muffins

Picture opposite

Here is our version of a classic American favourite. Every time I eat one I can understand their popularity! Keep a packet of blueberries in your freezer, so you can make a batch of these at short notice.

1 cup baking bran (wheat bran)
1/4 cup wheatgerm or extra bran
1/2 cup canola oil
1 cup plain or fruity yoghurt
1 large egg

3/4 cup Champion Wholemeal Flour
3/4 cup Champion High Grade
    or Standard Plain Flour
1 tsp cinnamon
1 tsp Edmonds Baking Powder
3/4 tsp salt
1/2 tsp Edmonds Baking Soda
1 cup brown sugar
1–1 1/2 cups frozen blueberries (150–180g)

Measure the first five ingredients into a medium-sized bowl, mix to blend everything with a fork, then leave to stand. (If you don't have wheatgerm in the house, replace it with extra bran.)

Measure the remaining dry ingredients into a large bowl, and stir well with a fork to mix thoroughly.

Do not thaw the blueberries, but separate any clumps of berries. (We use half a 350g packet and find that this is a very good amount for this recipe, although you can use less.) Tip them onto the dry ingredients with the liquid mixture, then fold everything together until the dry ingredients are moistened.

Spoon the mixture into 12–15 medium or about 30 mini-muffin pans which have been buttered or sprayed.

Bake at 200°C for about 15 minutes, for longer than most other muffins, because of the frozen berries in the mixture, until centres spring back when pressed. (Read baking details on page 7.)

YIELD: 12–15 medium or 30 mini-muffins. **SERVE:** Warm or reheated, without any spread, at any time of the day.

Overnight Bran Muffins

If you enjoy your muffins hot from the oven, but don't want to spend any longer in the kitchen than necessary, stir together this mixture on Thursday or Friday night and cook it as required during the weekend.

For 30 medium muffins:
3 cups Champion Standard Plain Flour
3 cups baking bran (wheat bran)
1½ cups sugar
2 tsp cinnamon
2 tsp Edmonds Baking Soda
1 tsp salt
1 cup Californian raisins, sultanas
    or chopped walnuts or a mixture

1 cup canola oil
2 large eggs
1 cup plain or fruity yoghurt
2½ cups milk

Measure the first six ingredients into a large mixing bowl. Add the fruit or nuts (or a mixture of both) and toss well to mix the fruit and nuts with the dry ingredients.

In a medium sized bowl stir together the oil, eggs, yoghurt and milk with a fork until everything is well combined.

Pour the liquid onto the dry ingredients in the large bowl. Taking care not to overmix, fold the two mixtures together until the flour has been dampened. (For details of mixing and baking see page 7.)

Cook immediately or cover and refrigerate overnight or for up to 4 days. When required spoon as much mixture as required into lightly buttered or well sprayed muffin pans, or pleated paper liners. Avoid stirring the mixture before or after this process. Refrigerate remaining mixture promptly.

Bake at 200°C for 12–15 minutes or until the centre of each muffin springs back when pressed.

YIELD: About 30 medium-sized muffins. SERVE: Hot or warm, for breakfast and morning tea or coffee. Nice spread with cottage cheese and jam or jelly.

Oaty Refrigerator Low-Fat Muffins

Treacle gives these muffins a rich flavour, as well as enough colour to enable them to be microwaved. You can refrigerate the uncooked mixture for a week if you like just a few freshly baked muffins each day.

1/2 cup treacle
1 1/2 cups baking bran (wheat bran)
1 cup boiling water

1 cup brown sugar
2 Tbsp wine vinegar
1 tsp salt
2 large eggs
2 cups milk

2 cups Champion Standard Plain Flour
1 cup rolled oats
1 cup oat bran
1/2 cup wheatgerm
1 1/2 tsp Edmonds Baking Soda

Measure the treacle and bran into a large bowl. Pour over the boiling water and mix until combined. Cool for about 5 minutes. Add the sugar, wine vinegar, salt, eggs and milk and beat well with a fork.

In another bowl toss together the next five ingredients with a fork, to mix them well. Tip in the liquid ingredients and fold everything together, stirring only enough to combine. Cover and refrigerate over-night or up to a week before baking.

Without further mixing, spoon mixture, as required, into lightly buttered or well sprayed muffin trays. Bake at 200°C for 10–15 minutes or until the centres spring back when pressed. Refrigerate unused mixture promptly.

To microwave 4 muffins, spoon 1/4 cup of mixture into Teflon lined glass ramekins, cover with cling film pierced with several holes and cook on Full Power for 2 minutes or until firm.

NOTE: Microwaved muffins have their limitations, but they are convenient when only a few muffins are required.

YIELD: About 30 muffins. SERVE: Serve warm, soon after cooking, for breakfast, morning coffee or brunch.

Apple, Oat & Raisin Muffins

Apple sauce or puree, sultanas, seeds and spices give these muffins substance, as well as an interesting (but not too dense) texture and delicious flavour. A lemon glaze makes them irresistible.

2 cups Champion Wholemeal Flour
½ cup oat bran
½ tsp Edmonds Baking Soda
2 tsp Edmonds Baking Powder
¾ tsp salt
2 tsp cinnamon
½ cup brown sugar
1 cup sultanas or Californian raisins
½ cup pumpkin or sunflower seeds

300g can (1 cup) apple sauce*
½ cup fruity yoghurt
¼ cup canola oil
1 large egg

Measure the first nine (dry) ingredients into a large bowl and stir well to combine. (For best flavour toast sunflower seeds before use, under a grill or in a dry frypan over moderate heat until they brown lightly and pop.)

In another bowl, whisk together the apple sauce, yoghurt, oil and egg. (*Replace apple sauce with tightly packed, pureed raw apple made by processing unpeeled quartered apples, if preferred.)

Fold the liquid ingredients into the flour mixture taking great care not to over-mix. Stop as soon as all the flour is moistened. (Towards the end of the mixing, add milk, orange juice or other fruit juice if the mixture seems firmer than a normal muffin mixture.)

Pile the mixture into 12 lightly oiled or sprayed muffin pans. (Pans will be filled more than usual, but this is not a problem.) Bake at 200°C for 12–15 minutes, or until firm when pressed in the centre.

OPTIONAL: For a delicious crunchy lemon glaze, brush all surfaces of hot muffins, when removed from their pans, with ¼ cup each of lemon juice and sugar, stirred but not heated together.

YIELD: 12 - 15 medium muffins. SERVE: Good warm or cold with coffee, etc. These make popular and healthy additions to lunch boxes and tramping packs.

Maple Walnut Muffins

My husband rated these muffins the best that have ever come out of our kitchen! I was especially pleased because they had been formulated to contain almost no cholesterol. This obviously did not affect their flavour and quality!

1½ cups Champion Wholemeal Flour
1 cup All-Bran type cereal*
1 cup walnut pieces
½ cup brown sugar
½ tsp Edmonds Baking Soda
1 tsp Edmonds Baking Powder
¾ tsp salt

½ cup maple syrup
½ cup canola oil
½ cup natural low-fat yoghurt
1 large egg or 2 egg whites

*We used an extruded mixed bran cereal as our first choice, and extruded wheat bran (All-Bran) when this was not available.

Measure the flour, bran cereal, walnut pieces and sugar into a large bowl. Sift in the baking soda, baking powder and salt then stir until evenly combined.

Combine the syrup, oil, yoghurt and egg (or egg whites) in another bowl and whisk to combine. Pour the liquid mixture into the dry ingredients and fold everything together. Take care not to overmix (see mixing and baking details on page 7).

Spoon the mixture into 12 lightly sprayed or oiled muffin pans and bake at 200°C for 12 minutes or until firm when pressed in the centre.

NOTES: The maple syrup may cause these muffins to brown quickly and darken too much if they are cooked too long or at too high a temperature. Reduce heat if necessary when cooking with fan-forced air.

Use "Real" or maple "flavoured" syrup.

For NO cholesterol muffins replace the yoghurt with no-fat milk or fruit juice, and use egg whites instead of whole egg.

YIELD: 12 generous medium-sized muffins. SERVE: Anytime, with tea or coffee.

Best Banana Bran Muffins

Alison often makes these during her cooking shows, to prove that muffins which contain no butter or oil as well as a lot of bran can be moist and taste absolutely delicious. See for yourself!

2 cups baking bran (wheat bran)
½ cup sultanas
½ cup chopped nuts
½ cup Champion Standard Plain Flour
1 tsp Edmonds Baking Powder
1 tsp Edmonds Baking Soda
1 tsp cinnamon

½ cup golden syrup
1 cup milk
1 large egg or 2 egg whites*
2 large bananas, mashed

Measure the bran into a large bowl. Add the sultanas and nuts. Measure the flour, baking powder, baking soda and cinnamon into a sieve over the bowl, shake them onto the bran and stir to mix evenly.

Warm the tin of golden syrup in a bowl of hot water until it is runny, then measure what you need into a bowl, using a hot, wet measuring cup for ease. Add the milk and egg and beat with a fork until well mixed. Mash the bananas with a fork, on a board or plate, and stir into the liquid.

Tip the liquid mixture into the dry ingredients and fold together just until bran is evenly dampened. Do not overmix! (See page 7 for mixing and baking details.)

Divide the mixture evenly into the well sprayed muffin pans using two spoons.

Bake at 200°C for about 7 minutes for mini-muffins and 10 minutes for larger muffins, or until muffins spring back when pressed in the middle. Watch carefully during cooking, since muffins containing a lot of golden syrup burn easily. Leave for 2–3 minutes before twisting and removing from pans.

*For diets excluding egg yolks, use two large egg whites instead.

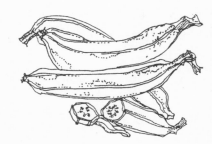

YIELD: 18 medium or 36 mini-muffins. **SERVE:** Eat warm, freezing extras. Spread large muffins with low fat cottage cheese. Serve mini-muffins plain.

Carrot & Pineapple Muffins

These muffins taste so good that you may well make your reputation as a "Marvellous Muffin Maker" with them!
It is worth keeping a small can of pineapple on hand so that you can make them at any time.

2 cups Champion Wholemeal Flour
4 tsp Edmonds Baking Powder
¾ cup brown sugar
2 tsp cinnamon
1 tsp mixed spice
½–1 tsp salt
½ cup chopped walnuts

1 150g carrot, grated (1 cup)
1 small (227g) can crushed pineapple
¼ cup orange juice
1 large egg
¼ cup canola oil or 50g butter

Measure the first seven ingredients into a large bowl. Use the larger amount of salt if you are using oil rather than butter. Mix well using your hands, making sure that there are no large lumps of sugar in the mixture.

Grate the carrot. (If you are not sure of the quantity, weigh the carrot before grating it, or pack the grated carrot firmly into a cup measure.) Mix the grated carrot, all the contents of the can of crushed pineapple, the orange juice and egg together in another bowl. Stir in the oil or melted butter, then add this liquid to the flour mixture.

Fold everything together, until the flour is just moistened. Take care to avoid overmixing. Add a little extra juice if the mixture seems thicker than usual. (Read the mixing and baking details on page 7.)

Spoon the mixture into 12 or 24 sprayed or buttered medium or mini-muffin pans. Bake at 200°C for 12–15 minutes, or until the muffins spring back when pressed in the middle.

OPTIONAL: As soon as you have taken them from their pans, brush all their surfaces with a mixture of ¼ cup each of lemon juice and sugar.

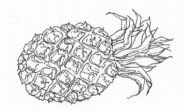

YIELD: 12 medium muffins or 24 mini-muffins. **SERVE:** Extra good straight from the oven or reheated.
Pack frozen mini-muffins in children's lunch boxes.

Jalapeno, Coriander & Corn Muffins (Wheat-Free)

Muffins made without wheat flour have a slightly different texture, but these interesting, well-flavoured cornmeal muffins disappeared remarkably fast - before they cooled in fact – so the difference was obviously not a worry.

2 cups grated tasty cheese
2 cups fine yellow cornmeal*
1 tsp Edmonds Baking Soda
2 tsp cream of tartar
¾ tsp salt
1 tsp ground cumin
2 Tbsp chopped fresh coriander leaves
1–2 Tbsp chopped (bottled) Jalapeno
   pepper

2 large eggs
¾ cup milk

Measure the grated cheese and cornmeal into a large bowl. Sift in the baking soda, cream of tartar, salt and ground cumin. Toss well to combine, then add the finely chopped coriander leaves and Jalapeno peppers, using the larger amount for spicier muffins.

Whisk the egg and milk together until lightly coloured and frothy on top. Add this immediately to the dry ingredients and mix until evenly combined.

Spoon into 12 sprayed or buttered muffin pans, sprinkle with a little paprika and bake at 200°C for about 12 minutes, until lightly browned and firm when pressed in the centre. (See baking details on page 7.)

* Use cornmeal which is as finely ground as flour, and which is a soft gold colour.

YIELD: 12 medium-sized muffins, slightly more compact than normal. **SERVE:** Serve warm or reheated. Especially useful for those on wheat-free diets.

Double Chocolate Muffins (Wheat-Free)

These wheat-free muffins make a treat for anybody who cannot eat a chocolate cake made with flour, and will be enjoyed by everyone in the family. They can be "dressed up" for a party, too.

1 cup rice flour
1/4 cup cocoa
1/2 tsp Edmonds Baking Soda
1/2 tsp salt
1 cup castor sugar

2 eggs, separated
1 cup plain or fruit flavoured yoghurt
1/2 cup chocolate chips

Sift the rice flour, cocoa, baking soda and salt and half the sugar into a large bowl.

Separate the eggs, putting the whites into a clean glass or metal bowl, and mixing the yolks with the yoghurt in another container.

Using an electric or hand beater, beat the egg whites until their peaks turn over when the beater is lifted from them, then add the remaining sugar and continue to beat until they will again form peaks that turn over.

Stir the egg yolk and yoghurt mixture into the dry ingredients then fold in a third of the beaten egg whites. Gently fold in the remaining egg whites and the chocolate chips. This should make a very soft, light batter.

Spoon the batter into 12 well-sprayed or buttered muffin pans and bake at 200°C for 12–15 minutes until firm when pressed in the centre. (For baking details see page 7.)

...peaks which curl over...

YIELD: 12 medium-sized, slightly compact muffins. **SERVE:** Warm or cold. Cut out centres, fill with whipped cream for "fairy cakes" for wheat-free diets, if desired.

Sticky Butterscotch & Walnut Muffins

When you want to delight your family, whip up a batch of these "upside down" muffins and serve them warm from the oven.
It's amazing what an interesting topping can do for a perfectly plain muffin!

100g butter, melted
½ cup soft brown sugar
about ½ cup chopped walnuts

2 cups Champion Standard Plain Flour
4 tsp Edmonds Baking Powder
½ tsp salt
¾ cup sugar

100g butter
1 large egg
1 cup milk

Lightly spray or butter the muffin pans. For the topping, measure into the prepared pans about two teaspoons each of melted butter, brown sugar and chopped walnuts. Press this down evenly.

Thoroughly mix the dry ingredients together in a large bowl, using a fork.

Melt the second measure of butter, then add the egg and milk and beat together lightly with a fork until well combined.

Fold together the two mixtures, taking care not to overmix! (See mixing and baking details on page 7.)

Using two spoons, carefully drop the mixture into the pans containing the topping ingredients.

Bake at 220°C for 10–12 minutes, or until the centres spring back when pressed.

The tops are likely to be flat rather than rounded.

Leave muffins to stand for 2 minutes before gently rotating them in their pans, to make sure that the topping is attached to them before you lift them out. BEWARE! The topping is very hot! Put muffins, topping up, on a rack or in a napkin-lined basket.

NOTE: If muffins are lifted out too soon, or left to stand for too long, the topping will remain in the pans.

YIELD: 12 medium muffins. **SERVE:** Warm or reheated. Allow to cool just enough to avoid burnt lips or mouths!

Macadamia & White Chocolate Muffins

These "All White" or "White Christmas" special occasion muffins are rich and cakey with a delicious vanilla flavour. They may look plain on the outside, but inside they are full of chunky pieces of white chocolate and macadamia nuts.

2 cups Champion Standard Plain Flour
3 tsp Edmonds Baking Powder
1 cup sugar
½ cup (75g) chopped Macadamia nuts
¾ cup (100g) chopped white chocolate

100g butter
1 cup milk
1 large egg
2 tsp vanilla

Measure the flour, baking powder and sugar into a large bowl. Add the chopped macadamia nuts and chopped white chocolate, then mix well with a fork to combine.

Melt the butter, then add the milk, egg and vanilla and beat with the fork until thoroughly blended.

Pour the liquid into the flour mixture and gently fold together until the flour is moistened. Do not overmix (see mixing and baking details on page 7).

Spoon the batter into 12 sprayed or lightly buttered, medium-sized muffin pans or 24 mini-muffin pans, and bake at 200°C for about 12 minutes, until golden brown and firm when pressed in the centre.

NOTE: We used best quality roasted, salted macadamia nuts (which we had bought for nibbling) when we made these. They were excellent for both purposes!

YIELD: 12 medium or 24 mini-muffins. (Small muffins are good since these are rich.) SERVE: Unbuttered only slightly warm or cold, with coffee or for dessert. Great for gifts.

Glazed Gingerbread Muffins

These muffins may not be as dark in colour as traditional gingerbread, but the combination of fresh root ginger and gingerale gives them a definite ginger flavour. They are good as is, but are particularly delicious when glazed.

2 cups Champion Self-Raising Flour
½–¾ cup sugar
1 Tbsp grated fresh root ginger
1 tsp mixed spice
1 tsp cinnamon

50g melted butter
1 cup gingerale
1 large egg

Optional Glaze
2 tsp butter, melted
1 tsp ground ginger
2 tsp golden syrup
2 tsp water
¼ cup icing sugar

Measure the flour, sugar, ginger and spices into a large bowl and stir to combine evenly.

Melt the butter in another bowl, then add the gingerale and egg. Whisk lightly to combine.

Pour the liquid into the dry ingredients, then fold gently together until the flour is just moistened (see mixing and baking details on page 7). Spoon the mixture into 12 sprayed or buttered muffin pans and bake at 200°C for 12–15 minutes.

If using, prepare the glaze by mixing together all the ingredients while the muffins bake. Warm it to brushable consistency if necessary. As soon as the muffins are cooked, remove them from the pans and brush the glaze on their tops, using a pastry brush or (unused!) varnish brush, while still hot.

YIELD: Makes 12 medium muffins. **SERVE:** Best eaten the day they are made. Nice warm or reheated.

Double Chocolate Surprise Muffins

I invented this recipe for my little chocolate book, but it is too good to leave out of this muffin collection. Make it without the raspberry "surprise" if you like, but it won't be quite as good.

1¾ cups Champion Standard Plain Flour
4 tsp Edmonds Baking Powder
¼ cup cocoa
½ cup sugar
½ cup (100g) chocolate chips

75g butter
2 large eggs
¾ cup milk
¾–1 cup raspberry jam
extra chocolate chips

Sift or thoroughly stir the flour, baking powder and cocoa together into a medium-sized bowl. Add the sugar and chocolate chips and toss with a fork to mix.

Melt the butter until just liquid, then add the eggs and milk and beat with a fork until well combined and smooth. Pour the liquids into the dry ingredients and fold together, mixing as little as possible. Stop as soon as there are no pockets of flour left as overmixing spoils muffins. (See the mixing and baking instructions on page 7.)

Coat 12 medium muffin pans lightly with non-stick spray or butter, then half fill each pan by spooning about a tablespoon of the mixture into the prepared tins, using two spoons.

Using a damp teaspoon make a small hollow in each muffin and fill it with a teaspoon of jam. Divide the remaining mixture between the muffins ensuring that the jam is completely covered.

Sprinkle the muffins with extra chocolate chips and bake at 200°C for about 10 minutes or until the centres spring back when pressed. Leave to stand for several minutes before twisting and removing from the pans. Leave to cool on a rack.

YIELD: 12 medium muffins. **SERVE:** Warm for best flavour. For a quick dessert serve with lightly whipped cream and fresh strawberries.

Golden Orange Muffins

The wonderful golden colour of these muffins will brighten the coldest day. Our muffin recipes often undergo changes as we make them, and this recipe is no exception, since we vary the liquid and additions to suit what we have on hand.

1 orange (about 200g)
1 cup sugar
1 large egg
½ cup milk or orange juice
100g butter, melted

1½ cups Champion Standard Plain Flour
1 tsp Edmonds Baking Powder
1 tsp Edmonds Baking Soda
½ cup sultanas or chopped dates
½ cup chopped walnuts, optional

Cut the unpeeled orange into quarters then each quarter into four. Put the chopped orange (skin and flesh) and the sugar into a food processor and process with the metal chopping blade until the orange is very finely chopped. Add the egg, milk or juice and melted butter and process until combined.

Sift the dry ingredients into a large mixing bowl, tip in the orange mixture, sprinkle the sultanas or dates over it, add the nuts if using them, then taking care not to overmix, fold everything together, stopping as soon as the dry ingredients are dampened. (See mixing and baking details on page 7.)

Prepare 12 medium-sized muffin pans by buttering lightly or spraying with non-stick spray. Spoon mixture into the prepared pans, using two spoons.

Bake at 200°C for 12–14 minutes, until golden brown and until the centres spring back when pressed.

VARIATION: For Orange Cream Cheese Muffins leave out dried fruit and nuts. Half fill muffin pans with mixture, place a spoonful of cream cheese on the centre of each, then top with remaining mixture.

YIELD: 12 medium muffins. SERVE: Best warm. These don't need buttering.

Orange & Lemon Muffins

We almost called these "Bells of St Clemens" muffins, then decided against it! Whatever their name, however, these muffins should delight everybody who enjoys the clear, clean flavours of citrus fruit as we do.

2 cups Champion Standard Plain Flour
4 tsp Edmonds Baking Powder
½ tsp salt
¾ cup sugar

100g butter, melted
1 large egg
½ cup milk
1 orange, grated rind and juice
1 lemon, grated rind and juice
¼ cup sugar for glaze

Measure the first four ingredients into a bowl and toss lightly to mix thoroughly.

Melt the butter until just liquid. Add the egg and milk and mix with a fork until well combined. Grate all the coloured rind from the orange and lemon and stir into the butter mixture.

Squeeze the juice from the orange and add enough water to make it up to half a cup. (Do not squeeze the lemon until later.) Combine the three mixtures and fold together carefully until the flour is dampened. (See details on page 7.)

Spoon mixture into 12 sprayed or lightly buttered medium-sized muffin pans.

Bake at 200°C for 12 minutes or until the centres spring back when lightly pressed.

Stir the juice from the lemon with the sugar for the glaze. Brush this over all the surfaces of the hot muffins using a pastry brush, then cool on a rack.

VARIATIONS: Process the sugar and the thinly peeled orange and lemon rinds until very finely chopped. Add remaining dry ingredients and process briefly. Combine with remaining ingredients as above.

Make a cream cheese filling for these muffins as on opposite page, if desired.

YIELD: 12 medium-sized muffins. SERVE: Warm or reheated for brunch, lunch, with coffee or tea, or for dessert.

Glazed Passionfruit Muffins

— Picture opposite

These muffins are a special treat for lucky people growing their own black passionfruit, or those with a friend who grows enough to share! (If you freeze unsweetened pulp you can make these muffins out of season, too.)

50g butter, melted
½ cup sour cream
¼–½ cup fresh passionfruit pulp
up to ¼ cup orange juice
2 large eggs
¾ cup sugar

2 cups Champion Self-Raising Flour

Glaze
2 Tbsp passionfruit pulp
¼ cup icing sugar
   or 2 Tbsp bottled passionfruit in syrup

Melt the butter until liquid in a large bowl, then stir the sour cream into it.

Halve fresh passionfruit and scoop out all the pulp with a teaspoon. (Put aside two tablespoons to make the glaze.) You need at least ¼ cup of passionfruit in the muffins to get a good flavour. Add enough orange juice to make the pulp up to ½ cup. Add to the bowl.

Break the eggs into the bowl, add the sugar, then beat with a fork until well blended.

Sprinkle or sieve the flour on to the mixture in the bowl, then fold it in taking care not to overmix. (Read mixing and baking details on page 7.) Divide the mixture between 12 medium muffin pans which have been buttered or coated with non-stick spray.

Bake at 210°C for 10–15 minutes, until tops spring back when pressed.

While muffins cook, mix the reserved passionfruit pulp with the icing sugar to pouring consistency (or use bottled syrup). Brush the glaze over the muffins as soon as you take them from the oven.

VARIATION: Make Passionfruit Cream Cheese Muffins as in the variation on page 38.

YIELD: 12 medium muffins. **SERVE:** Preferably on the day they are made, cold or slightly warm, unbuttered, with tea or coffee.

Crunchy Lemon & Poppyseed Muffins

Picture opposite

I created these muffins after a holiday in California, where I was unable to resist a miniature lemon and poppyseed cake while grocery shopping. They taste every bit as good, although they are not nearly as rich as the cake was!

2 cups Champion Self-Raising Flour
1 cup sugar
½ cup poppyseeds
finely grated rind of 2 lemons

100g butter
2 large eggs
1 cup milk

juice of 2 lemons
¼ cup sugar

Measure the flour, sugar and poppyseeds into a large bowl. Finely grate in all the coloured rind from the lemons.

Heat the butter until just melted. Add the eggs and the milk and beat with a fork until everything is thoroughly combined.

Tip the liquid into the dry ingredients and fold together until the flour is dampened. Do not beat till smooth. For details of mixing and baking see page 7.

Spoon mixture into 12 medium-sized muffin pans which have been lightly buttered or sprayed.

Bake at 200°C for 10–15 minutes until golden brown, and until the centres spring back when pressed. While muffins cook, squeeze the lemon juice and mix with the second amount of sugar. (The sugar should not be dissolved.)

As soon as you take them from their pans, brush the lemon and sugar mixture over the tops of all the muffins, and the rest over their sides and bottoms. Cool on a rack.

VARIATION: Make Lemon, Poppyseed and Cream Cheese Muffins as in the variation on page 38.

YIELD: 12 medium muffins **SERVE:** Warm or reheated, with coffee, tea, for lunch or for dessert.

Pineapple, Orange & Ginger Muffins

Keep a small can of crushed pineapple in your store cupboard so you can make these muffins at any time. The ginger is optional but is a real treat for those (like me) who love it.

227g can crushed pineapple
¾ cup orange juice
1 large egg
100g butter, melted

2 cups Champion Standard Plain Flour
2 tsp Edmonds Baking Powder
½ tsp Edmonds Baking Soda
¾ cup brown sugar
about 8 pieces crystallised ginger

In a medium-sized bowl mix the first four ingredients (including the juice from the can) with a fork, until well combined.

Measure the flour, baking powder and baking soda into a large bowl. Stir in the brown sugar, removing any lumps, and add the thinly sliced or finely chopped crystallised ginger. Mix all this together thoroughly.

Tip in the combined liquid ingredients and stir only until the flour has been dampened, not until smooth. Do not overmix! (See the mixing and baking details on page 7.)

Divide the mixture evenly into 12 medium sized, lightly buttered or sprayed muffin pans. If you like a stronger ginger flavour, thinly slice a few extra pieces of crystallised ginger on top of the uncooked muffins.

Bake at 200°C for 10–15 minutes or until the centres spring back when lightly pressed. Leave to stand for a few minutes before twisting carefully to remove from the pans. Cool on a rack.

VARIATIONS: Leave out the ginger and/or replace the orange juice with milk.

Brush hot muffins with glaze given on page 46.

YIELD: 12 medium muffins. **SERVE:** Warm or cold, with coffee, at any time of day.

Rhubarb & Fresh Ginger Muffins

The tartness of rhubarb, the warm spiciness of fresh ginger and just a hint of orange combine to give these muffins a really special flavour which is surprisingly different.

2 cups Champion Standard Plain Flour
1 cup sugar
2 tsp Edmonds Baking Powder
½ tsp Edmonds Baking Soda

grated rind and juice of ½ orange,
    made up to 1 cup with milk
1 large egg
1 Tbsp grated fresh root ginger
1 cup finely sliced raw rhubarb
100g butter

In a large bowl mix the four dry ingredients thoroughly, using a fork.

Grate the rind from half an orange and squeeze its juice into a 1 cup measure. Add milk to make the liquid up to one cup. Tip into a bowl, add the rind, egg and the (fresh or frozen) grated ginger, and beat with a fork until well combined. Carefully stir in the rhubarb, sliced no more than 4 mm thick with a very sharp knife.

Tip the liquids into the dry ingredients and gently fold together, until the flour has just been moistened. Take care not to overmix. (See the mixing and baking instructions on page 7.)

Spoon the mixture evenly into well sprayed or lightly buttered muffin pans.

Bake at 220°C for 12–15 minutes, or until muffins spring back when pressed in the middle. Leave to stand for a few minutes before twisting and removing from the pans.

VARIATION: To glaze, brush hot muffins with the mixture used on page 36 or 46.

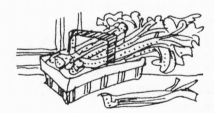

YIELD: Makes 12 medium muffins. SERVE: Warm, for a weekend breakfast, with tea or coffee at any time of day, or with lightly whipped cream for dessert.

Mango (or other fruit) Muffins

Try this useful recipe when you have ripe fresh fruit, but no specific muffin recipe using it. It works with well-drained canned fruit, too. Add spices if the fruit is not bursting with flavour. A large juicy mango makes great muffins!

2 cups Champion Standard Plain Flour
¾ cup sugar
4 tsp Edmonds Baking Powder
1 tsp cinnamon or mixed spice or freshly
    ground cardamom

75g butter
1 large egg
grated rind and juice of 1 orange
milk or extra juice
1–1½ cups cubed, ripe raw mango or
    other raw or canned fruit

Optional Topping
1 Tbsp sugar
½ tsp cinnamon

Mix the first three ingredients and the spice of your choice in a large mixing bowl, using a fork. (Cardamom is lovely with mango and peaches.)

In another container, heat the butter until liquid, then mix in the egg and finely grated orange rind with the fork.

Put the squeezed orange juice in a cup measure. Add any juice from the fruit you are using, or extra orange juice, or milk or yoghurt, to make up to ¾ cup.

Using a sharp (preferably serrated) knife, cut the fruit you are using into small 5–10 mm cubes. You should have about a cupful altogether.

Stir the fruit into the liquid mixture, then fold this into the dry ingredients, mixing just enough to dampen the flour. (See details on page 7.)

Spoon mixture into 12 or 24 buttered or sprayed medium or mini-muffin pans. Sprinkle with the second measures of sugar and cinnamon if desired.

Bake at 200°C for 12–15 minutes, until centres of muffins are firm when pressed.

VARIATION: Brush hot muffins with juice of 1 lemon mixed with ¼ cup sugar.

YIELD: 12 medium or 24 mini-muffins. SERVE: Warm or reheated, at any time of day, from breakfast to dessert.

Fabulous Feijoa Muffins

Why are these muffins fabulous? Well, even people who do not like feijoas keep reaching for yet another! Added orange rind and juice, and a cinnamon topping make the muffins really interesting, without overwhelming the feijoa flavour.

75g butter, melted
1 cup finely chopped feijoa flesh
2 large eggs
finely grated rind of 1 orange
¼ cup orange juice

¾ cup sugar
2 cups Champion Self-Raising Flour

1 tsp cinnamon
1 Tbsp sugar

In a large bowl, heat the butter until it is liquid.

Halve the feijoas and scoop out their centres with a teaspoon. (Muffins are nicest if you do not use much of the firmer outer shell.) Chop feijoa into pieces no bigger than peas. Pack into cup measure. Mix this into the melted butter, with a fork.

Add the unbeaten eggs, orange rind, and the juice of the orange made up to volume with a little lemon juice if necessary. Mix until everything is combined.

Sprinkle the sugar and the self-raising flour over the mixture in the bowl, and fold it in without overmixing. (If you have used too much firm feijoa flesh you may need to add a little extra juice or milk to reach usual muffin consistency.)

Divide the mixture between 12 medium or 24 mini-muffin pans which have been buttered or sprayed. (Read mixing and baking details on page 7.)

Mix the cinnamon and second measure of sugar, and sprinkle it on the muffins. Bake at 210°C for 10–15 minutes, until the centres spring back when pressed.

VARIATION: For Raspberry and Feijoa Muffins add an extra ¼ cup of sugar and fold in 1 cup of frozen raspberries.

YIELD: 12 medium or 24 mini-muffins. **SERVE:** Slightly warm for best flavour, at any time of day.

Spicy Peach (Butterscotch) Muffins

We love these muffins made with perfectly ripe, fresh peaches (or nectarines), but when these aren't on hand, we reach for a convenient can, especially if unexpected guests arrive. The butterscotch topping is optional but really yummy!

3 cups Champion Standard Plain Flour
2 tsp cinnamon
2 tsp mixed spice
½ tsp ground cloves
1 tsp Edmonds Baking Soda
½ tsp salt
1 cup sugar
½–1 cup sultanas, optional

410g can peach slices, drained
125g butter
2 large eggs
½ cup peach syrup or orange juice
¼–½ cup milk

Measure first eight ingredients into a large mixing bowl. Mix well with a fork.

Drain the peaches in a sieve over a bowl. Cut each peach slice in about four pieces. Keep ½ cup of peach juice to add later. (If using fresh fruit peel and chop, until you have 1 cup of chopped well-packed fruit.)

In another container melt the butter until liquid. Add the eggs, reserved peach syrup (or juice if you are using fresh fruit) and ¼ cup of milk and beat with a fork until mixed. Stir in the chopped fruit.

Tip this mixture, all at once, into the dry ingredients, then fold together, adding extra milk if necessary, until mixture is of muffin consistency. Do not overmix. (Read mixing and baking details on page 7.)

Spoon into lightly sprayed or buttered muffin pans and bake in batches at 220°C for 10–15 minutes, until the centres spring back when pressed.

Brush with butterscotch topping while hot, if you like. While muffins cook, heat 25 grams of butter with ¼ cup brown sugar until mixture feels smooth, then take off the heat and stir in ¼ cup of sour cream and ½ tsp vanilla.

YIELD: 18 medium muffins or 36 mini-muffins. **SERVE:** Warm, at any time of day.

Apricot, Almond & Coconut Muffins

We love this combination of flavours in muffins as long as the end result is soft and moist. We usually intensify the almond flavour with a few drops of essence, but if you think this overwhelms other flavours, leave it out!

75g dried apricots (½ cup finely chopped)
½ cup orange juice
½ cup fine desiccated coconut
¼ cup blanched almonds

75g butter
3–4 drops almond essence, optional
¾ cup milk
1 large egg
¾ cup sugar

1¾ cups Champion Self-Raising Flour

about 2 Tbsps of apricot jam, optional

Chop the dried apricots finely and heat in the orange juice in a microwave bowl or medium-sized pot until the juice boils. Add the coconut and the finely chopped almonds, and heat again for a minute or two, until all the liquid is absorbed, then remove from the heat.

Stir in the butter, cut in several cubes. Add the almond essence if you are using it. When the butter has melted, add the milk, egg and sugar and beat with a fork until the egg is mixed in evenly.

Sprinkle the flour on top of the mixture, then fold it in until no lumps remain, stirring no more than necessary. (See the mixing and baking details on page 7.)

Spoon into 12 buttered or sprayed medium sized muffin pans.

Bake at 210°C for 10–15 minutes, until tops are golden and the centres spring back when lightly pressed. Leave to stand for 3–4 minutes before twisting gently and removing from the pans.

Brush tops of muffins with heated apricot jam (thinned with a little orange juice if necessary) to glaze them if you like.

YIELD: 12 medium muffins. **SERVE:** These are very nice served warm rather than hot, with morning coffee, with afternoon tea, or for dessert.

Upside-Down Nectarine Muffins

Picture opposite

We experimented with these muffins in the middle of winter, using Californian nectarines. As they cooled, they looked so beautiful and smelt so appetising, we couldn't believe it - the kitchen really seemed filled with Californian sunshine!

50g (12 tsp) butter
½ cup (24 tsp) brown sugar
3 fresh nectarines

2 cups Champion Self-Raising Flour
¾ cup sugar
1 tsp mixed spice
¾ tsp salt

2 large eggs
¾ cup plain or apricot yoghurt
¼ cup oil
1 tsp vanilla

Spray or lightly butter 12 medium muffin pans. Melt the butter. Put a teaspoon of it in each pan, then add 2 teaspoons of brown sugar, spreading it evenly over the bottom.

Quarter the nectarines and cut each quarter into three slices. Arrange three slices on top of the butter-sugar mixture in each pan.

Measure the dry ingredients into a large bowl and stir well to combine.

In another bowl lightly beat together the eggs, yoghurt, oil and vanilla.

Gently fold the liquid mixture into the dry ingredients, stopping as soon as the flour is moistened. Spoon the batter into the nectarine lined pans, then bake at 200°C

for 12–15 minutes. (Muffins may be flat topped. This is not a problem!)

After 2 minutes standing, press down gently on each muffin and rotate about ½ a turn, then lift the muffins onto a rack. The topping usually lifts off with the muffin if you get it at the right stage – not too soon, and not too late. Reposition any fruit that stays in the pans.

YIELD: 12 medium muffins **SERVE:** Warm or reheated, within a few hours of cooking. Good at any time of day, from breakfast to dessert!

Coconut, Cherry & Cream Cheese Muffins

Picture opposite

Coconut cakes have long been popular in our family. Most loved was a coconut and cherry cake, so it was really only a matter of time before we used the same flavours in these absolutely delicious muffins!

1½ cups Standard Plain Flour
1 cup sugar
3 tsp Edmonds Baking Powder
½ tsp salt
1 cup fine desiccated coconut

½ cup cream cheese
¾ cup milk
1 large egg
¾ tsp vanilla essence
¼ tsp almond essence, optional
1 cup (150g) glacé cherries

Sift the flour, sugar, baking powder and salt into a large bowl. Add the coconut and toss together.

In a food processor, or by hand, beat together the cream cheese, milk, egg and essences (this will be easier if you soften the cream cheese by warming it first).

Fold the liquid mixture into the dry ingredients, stopping as soon as all the flour is moistened (see page 7 for mixing and baking instructions).

Spoon into 12 muffin pans, sprinkle with some long shreds of coconut if you have it, then bake at 200°C for 12 minutes, or until lightly browned and firm when pressed in the centre.

If desired, dust with icing sugar, or brush with apricot jam (see page 49).

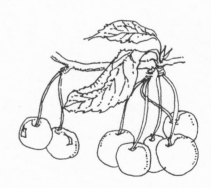

YIELD: 12 medium muffins. **SERVE:** Good cold or slightly warm, within two days of making.

Lemonade & Cream Muffins

These light textured, very easy (and very good) muffins are based on a scone recipe which "did the rounds" some time ago. For a summertime treat, serve them warm, split, with jam and/or fresh strawberries and whipped cream.

2 cups Champion Self-Raising Flour
1/2 cup sugar
1/4 tsp salt

1/2 cup lemonade
1/2 cup cream
1 large egg

Measure the flour, sugar and salt into a large bowl, and toss together with a fork. In another bowl, mix the lemonade, cream and egg with the fork, until combined.

Pour the liquid into the dry ingredients, then fold gently together until the flour is just moistened (see mixing and baking instructions on page 7). Spoon the mixture into 12 sprayed or buttered muffin pans.

Bake at 200°C for 10–15 minutes, until they are a light golden colour and firm when pressed in the centre.

YIELD: 12 medium muffins. SERVE: Best when freshly made, especially with whipped cream and fresh berries.

Easy Jaffa Muffins

These muffins, with an interesting orange tinge, are popular after school and at parties. They are simple enough for kids to make. The 12 year old in our family replaces the orange fizz with lemonade to make "Elizabeth's Dalmatian Muffins"!

2 cups Champion Self-Raising Flour
½–¾ cup sugar
¼–½ tsp salt
½ cup chocolate chips

¼ cup oil, preferably canola
1 cup orange "fizz" eg Fanta
1 large egg

Measure the flour, sugar, salt and chocolate chips into a large bowl and mix with a fork to combine. (Use the amount of sugar and salt that suits your taste.)

Put the oil, fizzy drink and egg into another bowl and whisk with the fork until mixed.

Pour the liquid into the dry ingredients, then fold gently together until the flour is just moistened (see mixing and baking instructions on page 7).

Spoon the mixture into 12 medium or 24 mini- muffin pans which have been well sprayed or oiled, and bake at 200°C for 10–15 minutes, or until firm when pressed in the centre.

YIELD: 12 medium or 24 mini-muffins. SERVE: As suggested above, the day they are made. Freeze extra muffins in plastic bags. Put them, frozen, in school lunches, to thaw during the morning.

Partytime Cola Muffins

We found that we could make interesting and colourful (if rather unusual!) fun muffins by baking sweets in this mixture! On a good day the resulting muffins lift out easily from unlined pans, but it may be safer to use paper cup-cake liners!

2 cups Champion Self-Raising Flour
1 cup sugar
¼ tsp salt

½ cup cream
½ cup cola
1 large egg
24 – 36 sweets (see list below)

Suitable sweets to use include Pebbles, Jaffas, soft fruit jubes, caramels, jelly babies (with their heads out) or chunks of dark, milk or white chocolate.

Using a fork, mix the flour, sugar and salt together in a large bowl.

Put the cream, cola and egg in another bowl, and mix with the fork until well combined.

Pour the liquid mixture into the dry ingredients, then fold everything together gently until the flour is just moistened (see mixing and baking instructions on page 7).

Spoon the mixture into 12–15 paper cup-lined (or well sprayed or buttered) medium muffin pans, or into 24 well-sprayed mini-muffin pans. Press two or three sweets into the medium muffins and one sweet into the mini-muffins, then push the mixture back over the top of the sweets.

Bake at 200°C for 10–15 minutes or until firm when pressed near the centre. (Do not press the sweets, since they get very hot.) Lift carefully out of sprayed pans after 2–3 minutes. Do not eat until the sweets cool down.

VARIATIONS: If you don't have any cream, make the muffin mixture on page 55.

For Rum and Cola muffins (for adults) make the muffins without sweets. Brush all surfaces of the cooked muffins, while very hot, with a mixture made by stirring together 2 Tbsp rum, 1 Tbsp lemon juice and ¼ cup sugar. Serve warm.

YIELD: 12 - 15 medium muffins or 24 mini-muffins. **SERVE:** to children, within an hour of making.

Peanut Butter & Jam Muffins

Peanut butter lovers of all ages are sure to enjoy these muffins! The jam makes them even more interesting. It is impossible to tell exactly how much milk is needed because peanut butters vary in solidity. Use your own judgment!

2 cups Champion Standard Plain Flour
3 tsp Edmonds Baking Powder
¾ tsp salt
½ cup brown sugar

½ cup peanut butter
¼ cup oil, preferably canola
1 cup milk
1 large egg

12 tsp (¼ – ½ cup) raspberry
or strawberry jam

Measure the flour, baking powder, salt and sugar into a large bowl and stir to combine, break up any lumps of brown sugar with your (clean) fingers.

Measure the peanut butter, oil, milk and egg into another bowl, then beat well with a fork or whisk to mix everything.

Pour the liquid mixture into the dry ingredients, then fold gently together until the flour is just moistened, mixing no more than necessary. If the mixture looks as if it will be thicker than muffin mixture usually is, add up to ¼ cup of extra milk. (Read mixing and baking instructions on page 7.)

Spoon mixture into 12 sprayed or buttered medium muffin pans or 24 mini-muffin pans. Using the back of a wet teaspoon make a deep depression in the top of each medium muffin and fill with a teaspoon of jam. (Alternatively, "inject" a little jam into the batter of medium or mini-muffins, using a forcing bag and nozzle or a "squeezy" nozzle-topped bottle.)

Bake at 200°C for 10–12 minutes, or until firm when pressed near the centre. Watch out not to touch the hot filling when taking the muffins from the pans. Let jam cool before eating.

YIELD: 12 medium or 24 mini-muffins. **SERVE:** Warm or reheated (but not too much) to children and other peanut butter lovers.

Moro Muffins

The addition of chopped Moro or Mars bars to these muffins makes them a hit with chocoholics of all ages.
Don't get too carried away with the amount you add though, or the muffins will tend to stick to the pans.

2 cups Champion Self-Raising Flour
¾ cup brown sugar
1 tsp cinnamon
¾ tsp salt

1 large egg
1 cup plain or apricot yoghurt
¼ cup oil
80–100g Moro or Mars bars, chopped

Measure the flour into a large bowl. Add the brown sugar, cinnamon and salt, then mix well to break up any lumps, using your fingers if necessary.

In another bowl combine the egg, yoghurt and oil. Stir these together with a fork until well combined.

Pour the liquid into the dry ingredients, add the chopped Moro or Mars bar and fold everything gently together until the flour is just moistened (see mixing and baking instructions on page 7).

Spoon the mixture into 12 sprayed or buttered muffin pans (or use paper liners to avoid possible trouble with sticking, later).

Bake at 200°C for 12–15 minutes, or until firm when pressed in the centre. Leave to cool for 1–2 minutes then remove from the pans. (BEWARE of burns from hot melted confectionery.)

YIELD: 12 medium muffins. **SERVE:** Warm, reheated (but not too much), or at room temperature, preferably the day they are made.

Caramel Surprise Muffins

These muffins are likely to be enjoyed by children (and adults!) who have a sweet tooth. Hidden in the middle of each delicious, mildly caramel flavoured muffin is a tasty caramel treat.

2 cups Champion Self-Raising Flour
½ cup brown sugar

50g butter
½ cup caramel (icecream) sauce
¾ cup milk
1 large egg
12 bought caramels or squares of homemade fudge (recipe on page 61)

Measure the flour into a large bowl. Add the brown sugar and mix well to break up lumps, using your fingers if necessary.

In another bowl, melt the butter, then add the (commercially made) caramel sauce, milk and egg. Stir with a fork until well combined.

Pour the liquid mixture into the dry ingredients, and fold gently together until the flour is just moistened (see mixing and baking instructions on page 7).

Spoon the mixture into 12 sprayed or buttered muffin pans, then press a piece of caramel into each cup. If you press the caramel well down the batter (not so far it touches the sides or bottom), the batter will rise and completely surround the caramel during baking.

Bake at 200°C for 12–15 minutes, or until firm when pressed in the centre. Remove from the oven and leave to stand for 2 minutes before removing from pans.

VARIATIONS: Omit the pieces of caramel – the muffins will still be good!

Use an extra ¼ cup of brown sugar and 1 tsp vanilla for sweeter muffins with a more marked caramel flavour.

YIELD: 12 medium muffins. **SERVE:** Best the day they are made, since the caramels harden on longer standing.

Modifying Muffin Recipes

There may be times when you want to make changes, substitutions or additions to our recipes. This might be to suit special dietary requirements, to fit in with your own personal eating pattern, to use the ingredients you have on hand, or to "dress up" your muffins!

We hope that the following guidelines, explanations and suggestions will help you to produce good results.

Wholemeal flour

Substitute up to half the regular (white) flour with wholemeal flour, or half the white self-raising flour with self-raising wholemeal, adding an extra tablespoon of liquid for each cup of wholemeal used.

High Grade flour

We used high grade flour instead of plain flour in some of our muffins since it has the ability to hold up other solid ingredients. If you don't have it on hand, use plain flour, which should give you results which are almost as good.

Non-dairy muffins

Use soy milk instead of milk, and soy yoghurt in place of yoghurt or sour cream. Replace butter with the same amount of dairy-free margarine or with oil. When using oil replace 50g butter with $\frac{1}{4}$ cup of oil, and add a little ($\frac{1}{4}$ tsp) salt.

Low cholesterol muffins

Replace 1 large egg with the whites of 2 large eggs. Use canola or light olive oil, or an olive oil based spread in place of butter, replacing 50g butter with $\frac{1}{4}$ cup of oil. You may want to add a little extra salt when replacing butter with oil. In many 2 egg muffin recipes you can leave out 1 egg altogether. Add 2–4 Tbsp of extra liquid instead.

Lower fat muffins

The butter or oil content of most muffin recipes can be reduced by half (or even more) by adding an equal volume of extra liquid (or fruit puree) in its place. The texture will not be exactly the same and the muffins should be eaten the day they are made, for best results. (Best Banana Bran Muffins use mashed banana and no butter or oil.)

Lower fat cheesy muffins

We bake cheese muffins at a high temperature to get an appetising golden-brown coloured crust and a good flavour. Replace grated cheese with quarter to half as much Parmesan cheese for a definite cheese flavour but less fat. Muffins which contain large amounts of cheddar cheese do not need added butter or oil as well.

Modifying Muffin Recipes

Frozen berries

We add frozen berries to muffins for convenience and because they do not stain the muffin batter as much as thawed berries. Muffins containing frozen berries take a few minutes longer to cook.

"Surprise" fillings

Some of our muffin recipes contain "surprise" fillings of teaspoons of jam and cream cheese. Experiment, adding these or lemon honey, Christmas mincemeat, pieces of chocolate or fudge etc., to other sweet muffins.

In savoury muffins, use well flavoured pestos or tapenade as "surprise" fillings or push small cubes of cheese into the tops of the uncooked muffins.

Glazed muffins

Check the index for details of the glazes we used on some muffins. Use them on other muffins, if you like. They give an attractive appearance and a lovely flavour.

Fabulous Fudge

Use this as a "surprise" filling.

100g butter
1 cup sugar
¼ cup golden syrup
400g can sweetened condensed milk
1 tsp vanilla

Mix all ingredients except vanilla in a flat bottomed casserole, or microwave bowl resistant to high heat.

Microwave on High for 10–12 minutes, stirring every 2 minutes until all sugar has dissolved, mixture has bubbled vigorously all over surface, and a little dropped in cold water forms a soft ball.

Add vanilla. Don't worry if the mixture looks slightly curdled or buttery. Beat with a wooden spoon for about 5 minutes, until mixture loses its gloss. Before it sets firm, spoon the mixture into a lightly buttered or sprayed 20cm square pan.

Refrigerate until firm, then cut into small cubes.

Index

Index

Knives

For about 20 years I have imported my favourite, very sharp' kitchen knives from Switzerland. They keep their edges well, are easy to sharpen, a pleasure to use, and make excellent gifts.

VEGETABLE KNIFE $8.00

Ideal for cutting and peeling vegetables, these knives have a straight edged 85mm blade and black (dishwasher-proof) nylon handle. Each knife comes in an individual plastic sheath.

BONING/UTILITY KNIFE $9.50

Excellent for boning chicken and other meats, and/or general kitchen duties. Featuring a 103mm blade that curves to a point and a dishwasher-proof, black nylon handle, each knife comes in a plastic sheath.

SERRATED KNIFE $9.50

I find these knives unbelievably useful and I'm sure you will too! They are perfect for cutting cooked meats, ripe fruit and vegetables, and slicing bread and baking. Treated carefully, these blades stay sharp for years. The serrated 110mm blade is rounded at the end with a black (dishwasher-proof) nylon handle. Each knife comes in an individual plastic sheath.

THREE PIECE SET $22.00

This three-piece set includes a vegetable knife, a serrated knife (as described above) and a right handed potato peeler with a matching black handle, presented in a white plastic wallet.

GIFT BOXED SET $44.00

This set contains five knives plus a matching right-handed potato peeler. There is a straight bladed vegetable knife and a serrated knife (as above), as well as a handy 85mm serrated blade vegetable knife, a small (85mm) utility knife with a pointed tip and a smaller (85mm) serrated knife. These elegantly presented sets make ideal gifts.

SERRATED CARVING KNIFE $28.50

This fabulous knife cuts beautifully and is a pleasure to use. The 21cm serrated blade does not require sharpening. Once again the knife has a black moulded, dishwasher safe handle and comes in a plastic sheath.

STEEL $20.00

The steel has 20cm blade and measures 33cm in total. With its matching black handle the steel is an ideal companion to your own knives, or as a gift. I have had excellent results using the steel. N.B. Not for use with serrated knives.

PROBUS SPREADER/SCRAPER $7.50

After my knives, this is the most used tool in my kitchen! With a comfortable plastic handle, metal shank and flexible plastic blade (suitable for use on non-stick surfaces), these are excellent for mixing muffin batters, stirring and scraping bowls, spreading icings, turning pikelets etc.

NON-STICK TEFLON LINERS

I regard these SureBrand Teflon liners as another essential kitchen item. They really help avoid the frustration of stuck-on baking, roasting or frying. Once you've used them, you'll wonder how you did without!

Round tin liner (for 15-23cm tins)	$6.50
Round tin liner (for 23-30cm tins)	$9.50
Square tin liner (for 15-23cm tins)	$6.50
Square tin liner (for 23-30cm tins)	$9.50
Ring tin liner (for 23cm tins)	$6.50
Baking sheet liner (33x44cm)	$13.95

All prices include GST. Prices current at time of publishing, subject to change without notice. Please add $3.50 post & packing to all orders (any number of items).

Make cheques payable to Alison Holst Mail Orders and post to: Alison Holst Mail Orders
Freepost 124807
PO Box 17016
Wellington

Or, visit us at www.holst.co.nz